2nd edition

openMind

Workbook

Ingrid Wisniewska

Concept development:
Mariela Gil Vierma

Level 2b

Macmillan Education
4 Crinan Street
London N1 9XW
A division of Macmillan Publishers Limited

Companies and representatives throughout the world

ISBN 978-0-230-45945-8 with key

Text, design, and illustration © Macmillan Publishers Limited 2014
Written by Ingrid Wisniewska
The author has asserted her rights to be identified as the author of this work in accordance with the Copyright, Designs, and Patents Act 1988.

This edition published 2014
First edition published 2010

All rights reserved; no part of this publication may be reproduced, stored in a retrieval system, transmitted in any form, or by any means, electronic, mechanical, photocopying, recording, or otherwise, without the prior written permission of the publishers.

Designed by emc design limited
Illustrated by Peter Cornwell p42 (Ex 5A); Sally Elford pp41, 69; Niall Harding (Beehive Illustration) p42 (Ex 4C); Paul Williams (Sylvie Poggio Artists) pp51, 54, 57, 73.
Cover design by emc design limited
Cover photograph by Getty Images / Blue Jean Images
Picture research by Alison Prior

Author's acknowledgements
The author would like to thank the schools, teachers and students whose input has been invaluable in preparing this new edition. She would also like to thank the editorial and design teams at Macmillan for doing such a great job of organizing the material and bringing it to life.

The publishers would like to thank the following educators and institutions who reviewed materials and provided us with invaluable insight and feedback for the development of the *openMind* series:

Carolina Ezeta, Universidad Tecnológica de Querétaro; Karl Schmack, Centro Cultural Costarricense Norteamericano; Maria Elisabeth Schmid de Mattos, ICBEU – São José dos Campos; Martha Patricia Sánchez, Colegio Anahuac Revolución; Leigh Darlaine Langenegger, ICBEU – São José dos Campos; Ricardo Pizelli Goiatá, Curso Bridge over Cam; Franklin Téllez, Centro Cultural Nicaragüense Norteamericano; Jim Nixon, Colegio Cervantes Costa Rica; Rosario Mena, Instituto Cultural Dominico Americano; Leticia de la Peña, Colegio Lincoln; Héctor Sánchez, PROULEX; Eric Tejeda, PROULEX; Arturo Hernández, Instituto Tecnológico de Estudios Superiores de Monterrey, Campus Guadalajara; Grisel del Rosario, Instituto Cultural Dominico Americano; Maria do Socorro Guimarães, IBEU – Rio de Janeiro; Diego Medina, Universidad de Guadalajara, Licenciatura de Idiomas; Julio Prin, Centro Venezolano Americano; María Guadalupe Muñoz, Universidad de Guadalajara, Licenciatura de Idiomas; Lourdes Molleda, Tec Milenio; Frances Gritzewsky, Prepa Tec Eugenio Garza; Magneli Villanueva Morales, Universidad Regiomontana; Anderson Lopes Siqueira, ICBEU – São José dos Campos; Emilia Rubenova, Universidad Autónoma de Nuevo León; Lourdes Pérez Valdespino, Universidad Del Valle de México, María Eugenia Rodríguez, Centro Cultural Salvadoreño Americano; Márcia Soares Guimarães, Instituto Cultural Brasil Estados Unidos -Belo Horizonte; Leonor Rosales, Instituto Tecnológico de Estudios Superiores de Monterrey; Martha Larraga, Unitec Escobedo; Cândido Prado, CCBEU – Goiânia; Janet Keyser, Instituto Tecnológico de Estudios Superiores de Monterrey, Campus Cuidad de México; Julie Khatcherian, Manhattan Trade Language Company; Francisco Nieto, Universidad Metropolitana; Artemisa Sangermán, Instituto Tecnológico de Estudios Superiores de Monterrey, Campus Cuidad de México; Nico Wieserma, Instituto Tecnológico de Estudios Superiores de Monterrey, Campus Cuidad de México; Vagner Serafim, Centro Cultural Brasil Estados Unidos; Lourdes Baledón, Universidad Intercontinental; Clara Lucía López, Centro Colombo Americano Manizales; Gabriela Rodríguez, Colegio Oviedo Schontal; Waldo Andrade, CBI: Centro Butantã Idiomas – São Paulo; Anthony Shull, Instituto Tecnológico de Estudios Superiores de Monterrey, Campus Estado de México; Tamara Rojas, Escuela Benjamín Franklin; Martha Rosas, Universidad del Valle de México, Campus San Rafael; Fabiano Cella, Universidade de São Paulo, curso Poliglota; Sheila Moreno, Universidad del Valle de México, Campus Tlalpan; Patricia Venegas, Universidad del Valle de México, Campus Lomas Verdes; Luciana Guarnier, Seven Idiomas; Diana Jones, Angloamericano; Carlos Lizárraga, Angloamericano; Emma Domínguez, The Anglo; Luis Cabrera, Universidad Nacional Autónoma de México; Luciane Oliveira, New York School; Cristina Moya, Colegio Morelos; Elda Beraza, Colegio Montes de Oca, Cuernavaca; Elza Massae Sato, FMU, São Paulo; Lucía Canseco Campoy, Instituto Tecnológico de Estudios Superiores de Monterrey, Campus Hermosillo; Emma Luisa Domínguez Instituto Tecnológico de Estudios Superiores de Monterrey, Campus Obregón; Yolanda Domínguez del Instituto Tecnológico de Estudios Superiores de Monterrey, Campus Obregón; Maria Antonieta Gagliardi, Centro Britânico – São Paulo; David Toledo, Universidad Autónoma de Baja California; Alicia Cabrero, Universidad Autónoma San Luis Potosí; Danielle Sales, Senac – Rio de Janeiro; Claudio Barros, Flex Idiomas; Rina de Góngora, del Instituto Guatemalteco Americano; Adriana Alcalá, Kate Cory-Wright, Chris Bauer; Moisés Ramírez; Universidad Chauhtémoc Centro de Lenguas y Lingüística Aplicada, Universidad Autonoma de Tamaulipas; Instituto Tecnológico Centro Americano; CELE Mascarones; Ministerio de Educación de El Salvador; Universidad Tecnológica de Nezahualcoyotl; Universidad del Tepeyac; Instituto Politécnico Nacional ESIME CELEX; Instituto Quebec; Colegio La Salle del Pedregal; Universidad Pedagógica Nacional; Universidad de la República Mexicana; Universidad Norteamericana; Fundación Empresarial para el Desarrollo Educativo; Operadora La Salle; Seven São Paulo; Universidad de Oriente; UNIVA; Centro de Capacitación Manuel Sandoval Vallarta; Universidad de El Salvador; Escuela de Jurisprudencia; Universidad de Valle de México, Campus Puebla; Alumni São Paulo; Dr. Amany Shawkey, Mrs. Heidi Omara, Mrs. Hala Fouad (Egypt); Faisal Mreish (Lebanon); Mrs. Magda Giomazi (Libya).

Petra Florianová, Gymnázium, Praha 6, Arabská 14; Inés Frigerio, Universidad Nacional de Río Cuarto; Alison Greenwood, University of Bologna, Centro Linguistico di Ateneo; Roumyana Yaneva Ivanova, The American College of Sofia; Táňa Jančaříková, SOŠ Drtinova Prague; Mari Carmen Lafuente, Escuela Oficial de Idiomas Hospitalet, Barcelona; Alice Lockyer, Pompeu Fabra University; Javier Roque Sandro Majul, Windmill School of English; Paul Neale, Susan Carol Owens and Beverley Anne Sharp, Cambridge Academy of English; Audrey Renton, Dubai Men's College, Higher Colleges of Technology, UAE; Martin Stanley, British Council, Bilbao; Luiza Wójtowicz-Waga, Warsaw Study Centre; Escuela Oficial de Idiomas de Getxo; Cámara de Comercio de Bilbao; Universidad Autónoma de Bellaterra; Escuela Oficial de Idiomas EOI de Barcelona; University of Barcelona; Escuela Oficial de Idiomas Sant Gervasi.

The authors and publishers would like to thank the following for permission to reproduce their photographs:
Alamy/The Art Archive p66(tl), Alamy/Roman Bayle p64(4), Alamy/Bon Appetit p43(r), Alamy/Chris Deeney p48, Alamy/Everett Collection p66(tc), Alamy/Gaba/G&B Images p64(2), Alamy/Hemis p56(tl), Alamy/D Hurst p45(tl), Alamy/Imagebroker p49, Alamy/ImageSource p52, Alamy/Jacques Jangoux p54, Alamy/Boris Karpinski p56(tc), Alamy/Fredrick Kippe p59(r), Alamy/Ian Middleton (bl), Alamy/Kasia Nowak p64(1), Alamy/David P G Philips p43(l), Alamy/PhotoAlto p71, Alamy/Charles Stirling p64(8), Alamy/Ken Tam p44(r), Alamy/Tetra Images p53(tr,bl); **Corbis** p75, Corbis/Toshiyuki Aizawa/Reuters p66(br); **Getty Images** pp40(cl&c), 45(cr), Getty Image/Adie Bush p60(t), Getty Images/AFP p66(bl), Getty Images/Christian Science Monitor p65, Getty Images/Cultura/Frank van Delft p60(b), Getty Image/David C Tomlinson p56(tr), Getty Image/Thomas Jackson p59(l), Getty Images/Jade p74, Getty Images/Howard Kingsnorth p72, Getty Image/Dimitri Otis p47; **Rex Features**/Zuma p66(tr); **Thinkstock** pp40(tr&cr), 44(l&c), 45(br, b, bc, bl, tr), 50, 53(tl), 55, 63, 64(3,5,6,7), 67, 68, 69(all), 70.

These materials may contain links for third party websites. We have no control over, and are not responsible for, the contents of such third party websites. Please use care when accessing them.

Printed and bound in Thailand

CONTENTS

UNIT 7 — A QUESTION OF TASTE — page 40

UNIT 8 — LOVE AND ROMANCE — page 46

UNIT 9 — OUR PLANET — page 52

UNIT 10 — PARTY ANIMALS — page 58

UNIT 11 — INNOVATE! — page 64

UNIT 12 — ACROSS THE GENERATIONS — page 70

AUDIO SCRIPT
page iv

ANSWER KEY
page vii

UNIT 7 A QUESTION OF TASTE

1 VOCABULARY: adjectives to describe food

A Complete the sentences with words to describe taste or texture.

1. Sugar isn't sour. It's _____.
2. Soy sauce isn't spicy. It's _____.
3. Lemons aren't sweet. They're _____.
4. Crackers aren't creamy. They're _____.

B Choose adjectives in the box to best describe the taste and texture of the food items.

creamy crunchy greasy juicy salty sour spicy sweet

1. apple   *crunchy* _____
2. mango   _____
3. cheese   _____
4. mustard   _____
5. ginger   _____
6. potato chips _____
7. grapefruit _____
8. ice cream _____

C 🎧 16 Listen to these people tasting different types of food. Write the words that describe each food. What is the mystery food?

1. Description _____ Mystery food _____
2. Description _____ Mystery food _____
3. Description _____ Mystery food _____
4. Description _____ Mystery food _____

2 GRAMMAR: too, enough, not ... enough

A Write the words in the correct order to make sentences.

1. creamy / enough / not / the / dessert / is / .
   _____
2. is / the / sauce / spicy / too / .
   _____
3. not / toast / is / crunchy / enough / the / .
   _____
4. the / ice cream / sweet / is / too / .
   _____

WATCH OUT!
✗ This coffee isn't enough hot.
✓ _____

B Rewrite the sentences using *too*, *enough*, or *not ... enough* and the adjective in parentheses.

1 This soup isn't hot enough. This *soup is too cold*. (cold)
2 This sauce doesn't need any more salt. This _____. (salty)
3 These French fries have a lot of oil. These _____. (greasy)
4 These grapes are too sour. These _____. (sweet)
5 This orange is too dry. This _____. (juicy)
6 These vegetables are too soft. These _____. (crunchy)
7 This lemonade doesn't need any more sugar. This _____. (sweet)

3 VOCABULARY: food containers

A Label the pictures with the name of the food and the correct container in the box.

| bag | bottle | box | can | jar | package |

1. a box of chocolates
2. _____
3. _____

4. _____
5. _____
6. _____

B Choose the correct option to complete the phrases.

1 a ... of ketchup
 a) can b) jar c) bottle
2 a ... of cereal
 a) can b) bottle c) box
3 a ... of flour
 a) package b) can c) bottle
4 a ... of lemonade
 a) box b) jar c) can
5 a ... of jam
 a) jar b) box c) can
6 a ... of cookies
 a) bottle b) package c) can

C 17 Chelsea and Yuki are planning a picnic. Listen and write their shopping list.

Food for the picnic
10 bags of potato chips

A question of taste   UNIT 7   41

4 GRAMMAR: quantifiers

A Complete the sentences with *too much*, *too many*, or *enough*.

1 You don't eat _____ vegetables. You should eat more.
2 You eat _____ potato chips. They aren't good for you.
3 Don't drink _____ lemonade. It has a lot of sugar.
4 Many people eat _____ junk food.
5 They don't eat _____ natural food.
6 I eat _____ cookies. They're not healthy!

B Read about these people's intentions to improve their diet. Complete the sentences with *less* or *fewer*.

Health and Mind Magazine

Five tips for a perfect diet

Here's what some of our readers are doing to improve their diets:

1 I want to lose weight, so I'm trying to eat _____ fried food and _____ fat, salt, and sugar.
2 Giving up cookies and chocolate is impossible! But at least I'm eating _____ cookies and _____ chocolate now.
3 I try to use _____ oil when I fry vegetables.
4 I'm trying to drink _____ cups of coffee—just one or two a day.
5 I'm going to eat _____ ice cream.

C Look at the picture and complete the note telling Harry what he needs to buy using quantifiers.

Hi Harry,
There isn't (1) _____ cheese and there's only a (2) _____ milk left. We only have a (3) _____ apples, and we definitely need (4) _____ grapes - there aren't (5) _____ at all! We have a (6) _____ of salad, though, so don't buy anymore of that.
Thanks!
Fiona

WATCH OUT!

✗ I don't drink many tea.
✓ _____

5 SPEAKING explaining what you mean

Match the descriptions 1–4 to the pictures A–D.

A ☐ B ☐ C ☐ D ☐

avocado   pomegranate   sushi   sweet potato

1 It's a type of fruit. It looks like an apple. It's red and yellow on the outside, and inside it has a lot of juicy seeds.
2 It's green. It's like a pear, but it isn't sweet. You can prepare it with salt and lemon juice.
3 It's like a potato, but it's orange. You can fry it in butter or bake it in the oven.
4 It's a kind of Japanese food. It's made with rice and seaweed, and it usually has fish or vegetables inside it.

6 READING: prediction

A Look at the title of the article and the picture in Exercise B. What do you think the article is about?

I think the article is about _____.

B Read the first paragraph of the article. Choose one option to predict the topic of the next paragraph. Then read the next paragraph to check. Continue in the same way with paragraphs two and three.

Chili cook-off

A chili cook-off is a popular social event in many cities and towns around the U.S.A. It's a competition to see who can make the best chili! A chili cook-off is a fun way to meet people, eat good food, and raise money for charity.

1 I think the topic of the next paragraph is going to be …
   a) the rules of a chili cook-off
   b) how to choose the best chili

A chili cook-off has a number of different rules. Visitors buy a button (the money goes to prizes and to charity). Each chef's name is a secret (so you can't vote for your friends). The visitors taste each dish and vote. Sometimes there are several prizes. For example, the most traditional, the most creative, or the spiciest chili. Anyone can enter the competition with their favorite chili recipe.

2 I think the topic of the next paragraph is going to be …
   a) types of chili dishes
   b) reasons to eat chili

The basic ingredients are onions, garlic, and, of course, chili peppers. Some people cook chili with beef, tomatoes, and beans. Others prefer a vegetarian version and add other vegetables such as green peppers and corn. Some like chili that is very spicy and hot. They include extra hot chilis as well as a lot of paprika. Every chef tries to have the best and most original recipe to win the cook-off.

C Now read the whole article again and choose the correct answers.

1. What is a *cook-off*? — a party / a competition / a national holiday
2. Who decides the winner of the cook-off? — friends / chefs / visitors
3. Does everyone have to use the same recipe? — yes / no / doesn't say

Listen and write

A 🎧 18 Listen to three people talking about the most unusual food they have ever tasted. Match the pictures to the speakers.

A – peanut butter and jam sandwich ☐

B – pickled herring on toast ☐

C – crocodile ☐

B Listen again and use key words to complete the table.

	Where did they eat it?	How do they describe it?	Did they like it?
1			
2			
3			

C Think about the most unusual food you have ever tried. Answer the questions.

1. What did you eat?

2. Where did you eat it?

3. What did it look/smell/taste/feel like?

4. Did you enjoy it?

Over to You

D ✏️ Use your answers from Exercise C to write a paragraph in your notebook about your unusual food experience.

WRITING TUTOR

The most unusual food I have ever tasted is …
I was in …

DOWN TIME

Food of the World

A Choose the one that doesn't belong.

1. Which food is not a fruit?   shrimp   banana   apple   orange
2. Which food is not made from milk?   cheese   yogurt   pasta   butter
3. Which one is not a fish?   tuna   salmon   herring   turkey
4. Which one is not vegetarian?   beans   steak   ketchup   spaghetti

B Choose the correct answer.

1. What kind of food do people eat in China to celebrate the New Year?
   a) eggs   b) noodles   c) carrots
2. What kind of food do people eat in the U.S.A. at Thanksgiving?
   a) turkey   b) beef   c) fish
3. On New Year's Eve in Spain, people eat …
   a) watermelon.   b) oranges.   c) grapes.
4. People in England eat Yorkshire pudding together with …
   a) beef.   b) toast.   c) cream.
5. What kind of food is caviar?
   a) frogs' legs   b) sharks' teeth   c) fish eggs
6. Parmesan is a type of cheese made in …
   a) Canada.   b) France.   c) Italy.
7. Sushi is a kind of Japanese food made from fish and …
   a) noodles.   b) rice.   c) bread.
8. In Japan, people often eat steamed rice with a pickled …
   a) cherry.   b) lemon.   c) plum.
9. In Mexico, a special sauce for chicken called "mole" is made with …
   a) chocolate.   b) seafood.   c) curry.
10. Chili is a kind of spicy stew made from meat, chili peppers, garlic, and …
    a) oranges.   b) onions.   c) broccoli.

A question of taste   UNIT 7   45

UNIT 8 LOVE AND ROMANCE

1 VOCABULARY: relationships

A Match the sentences A–E to the descriptions 1–5.

A We're going to get married!
B Will you have dinner with me?
C I don't want to see you anymore!
D I'll wear a red scarf so you'll recognize me.
E This is my girlfriend.

1. ☐ He's asking her out.
2. ☐ They're breaking up.
3. ☐ They're going out with each other.
4. ☐ They got engaged.
5. ☐ She's going on a blind date.

B 🎧 19 Complete the conversation. Then listen and check your answers.

A: Have Mike and Rachel (1) _____? I haven't seen them together recently.
B: Yes, Mike's (2) _____ with Julianna now. I think they just (3) _____.
A: Really? They haven't known each other that long, right?
B: No, they met on a (4) _____ about a month ago. The next day, he (5) _____ her _____ again, and the rest is history.
A: That's great news! I hope they'll be happy!

2 GRAMMAR: expressing likes, desires, and preferences

A Choose the correct option.

1. Would you like *see* / *to see* a movie tomorrow?
2. I'd rather not *eat* / *to eat* dinner too early.
3. Do you like *cook* / *cooking* Italian food?
4. Would you prefer *go out* / *to go out* to a restaurant or stay at home?
5. I'd like *go* / *to go* to a party this weekend.
6. Would you rather *have* / *to have* Mexican or Indian food tonight?
7. We'd prefer *cook* / *to cook* dinner at home.
8. Kyla likes *watching* / *watch* action movies.

B Write the words in the correct order to make sentences.

1. I / to / go / would / like / to / a party / .
   _____
2. for / would / like / you / to / go / dinner / out / ?
   _____
3. would / tonight / not / go / rather / we / out / .
   _____
4. home / prefer / you / would / to / eat / at / ?
   _____
5. not / eat / prefer / Italian / would / to / food / I / .
   _____
6. go / would / rather / you / a movie / to / ?
   _____

WATCH OUT!

 I'd rather not to see a movie tonight.

✓ _____

46

C What would you like to do on your first date? Write questions using the prompts. Then write true answers.

1 prefer / go to a movie
   A: *Would you prefer to go to a movie?*
   B: *No, I wouldn't.*
2 prefer / talk in a café
   A: _____
   B: _____
3 rather / meet with a group of friends
   A: _____
   B: _____
4 rather / go dancing
   A: _____
   B: _____
5 prefer / talk about music
   A: _____
   B: _____
6 would like / have dinner with your parents
   A: _____
   B: _____

3 GRAMMAR: gerund phrases as subject and object

A Underline the gerund in each sentence. Then check the correct option.

		Subject	Object	After a preposition
1	I'm thinking of having a party.	☐	☐	☐
2	Going to parties alone is pretty hard.	☐	☐	☐
3	I love dancing and listening to music.	☐	☐	☐
4	I'm good at talking to people at parties.	☐	☐	☐
5	I hate giving parties.	☐	☐	☐
6	Playing loud music at a party isn't a good idea.	☐	☐	☐

B Complete the paragraph with the gerund form of the verbs in the box.

| ask   chat   date   fill   get   give   go (x2)   make   meet |

Online dating is the perfect way to meet your ideal partner. **(1)** _____ out the registration is fast and easy—and best of all it's completely free. **(2)** _____ us details of your age, job, and interests will help us to search our database and find the perfect partner for you. It's easier than **(3)** _____ on a blind date. It's easier than **(4)** _____ someone out for the first time. **(5)** _____ to know a person online is a great way to find out if you are a perfect match! Most people are nervous about **(6)** _____ on their first date. **(7)** _____ online by text message or webcam before you meet are much better ideas! Our online service makes **(8)** _____ easy and fun! **(9)** _____ people and **(10)** _____ friends has never been easier!

WATCH OUT!

✗ I really enjoy go to parties.
✓ _____

Love and romance   UNIT 8

C Rewrite these sentences using a gerund.

1. It is easy to meet people at parties.
   _____ is easy.
2. It is fun to have dinner with friends.
   _____ is fun.
3. I feel sad when I argue with friends.
   I don't like _____.
4. I feel upset when I'm late for a meeting.
   I hate _____.
5. I never go out alone at night because I'm afraid.
   I'm afraid of _____.
6. He doesn't want to get engaged because he's nervous.
   He's nervous about _____.

4 WRITING: identifying paragraph structure

The sentences from two paragraphs are mixed up. Identify the sentences that go with each topic sentence. Write the sentence letters in the correct order below each topic sentence.

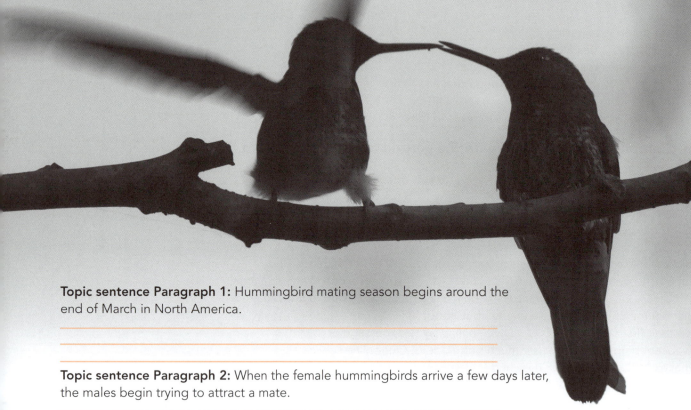

Topic sentence Paragraph 1: Hummingbird mating season begins around the end of March in North America.

_____

Topic sentence Paragraph 2: When the female hummingbirds arrive a few days later, the males begin trying to attract a mate.

_____

a) Males usually fly there from Mexico or Central America before the females.
b) It's important for the male to establish his territory around their mating place and guard it against intruders.
c) Other strategies include singing and flapping their wings as fast as possible to create a loud humming sound.
d) As soon as they arrive, they begin to look for a mating place.
e) The males fly high up into the air, and then dive straight down back toward the ground again.
f) The most important method of attracting the females is to fly around energetically.

5 LISTENING: understanding instructions and processes

A You are going to listen to a lecture about the Eastern Brown Pelican. First, read these statements and circle T (true) or F (false).

1 Pelicans reproduce once a year. T / F
2 The female lays only one egg. T / F
3 Male and female pelicans build nests together. T / F
4 Male pelicans do not incubate the eggs. T / F
5 Baby pelicans can talk to their parents from inside the egg. T / F
6 Only female pelicans can feed the babies. T / F

B 🎧 20 Now listen to the lecture and check your answers to Exercise A.

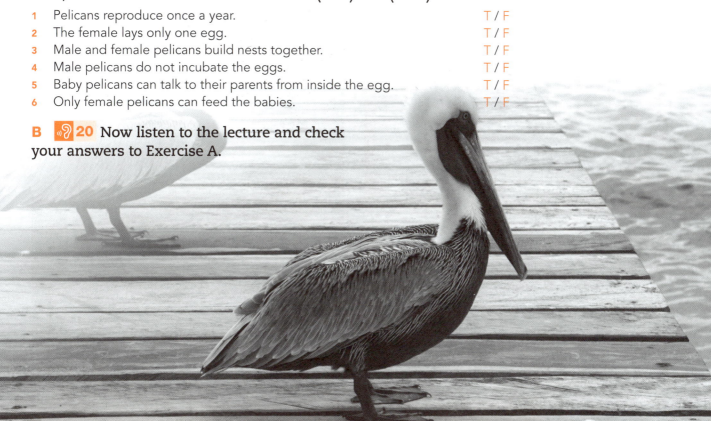

6 VOCABULARY: *get* + adjective

A Match the situations 1–6 to the consequences a–f.

1 Manuel got lost and couldn't find his friends.
2 Pete ate some uncooked chicken.
3 Martina broke her favorite vase.
4 Henry had nothing to do.
5 Yukiko had nothing to drink.
6 Adele ran a marathon.

a) She got angry.
b) He got bored.
c) He got worried.
d) She got thirsty.
e) She got tired.
f) He got sick.

B Complete the conversations with questions. Use *get* and a word in the box.

| angry   better   ~~hungry~~   sick   thirsty   tired |

1 **A:** We forgot to take food with us on our trip.
  B: *Did you get hungry?*

2 **A:** We spent eight hours hiking up a mountain.
  B: _____

3 **A:** I forgot my boyfriend's birthday.
  B: _____

4 **A:** We ate some berries and plants, but they weren't good.
  B: _____

5 **A:** My son had a bad cold and had to stay at home for four days.
  B: _____

6 **A:** We went bike riding, but left our water bottles at home.
  B: _____

Love and romance   UNIT 8   49

Read and write

A Read these people's descriptions of their first date. Then complete the table.

> On my first date, I went to a Chinese restaurant with a boy from school, and we ate noodles. I remember it was kind of hard to eat them with chopsticks, so I got shy and nervous, and only ate half of the food. He didn't seem to mind though, and afterward he asked me out again. I said yes, but on a first date, I'd prefer to eat Mexican food or pizza. (Gloria)

> I went on a blind date with a friend of my sister. We went bowling and I got bored, and I think she did, too. We didn't go on any more dates together after that. I'd rather go to a concert for a first date. (Takeo)

	What did they do on their first date?	How did they feel?	What would they prefer to do on a first date?
Gloria			
Takeo			

B Make notes about the first time you did something (your first date, your first driving lesson, your first visit to a foreign country…).

What did you do?	How did you feel?	Was it a good experience? Why or why not?

Over to You

C Use your notes in Exercise B to write a paragraph in your notebook about your experience.

WRITING TUTOR

I'll always remember the first time I …
I have never forgotten the first time I …
The first time I … was when I …
… was one of the best experiences of my life.

DOWN TIME

A Write a sentence below each picture of a stage in Tim and Sue's relationship. Then number them in the correct order.

☐ _____

☐ _____

☐ _____

☐ _____

☐ _____

☐ _____

B Read the clues. Complete the puzzle. Unscramble the letters. What's the mystery word?

1. I don't have any food. I'm _____.
2. I don't have any water. I'm _____.
3. The bus is late! I'm _____.
4. There's nothing on TV! I'm _____.
5. I was sick, but now I'm _____.
6. There's a spider! I'm _____.
7. We were engaged, and now we're _____.

Mystery word: _ _ _ _ _

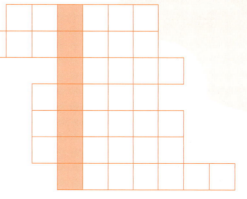

Love and romance   UNIT 8   51

UNIT 9   OUR PLANET

1 VOCABULARY: the weather

A Complete the sentences with words in the box.

foggy   rains   snows   stormy   sunny   windy

1 We usually go skiing when it _____.
2 The best time to fly a kite is when it is _____.
3 It's nice to sit on the beach when it is _____.
4 Sometimes there is thunder and lightning when it is _____.
5 You should drive carefully when it is very _____.
6 It's not much fun playing soccer when it _____.

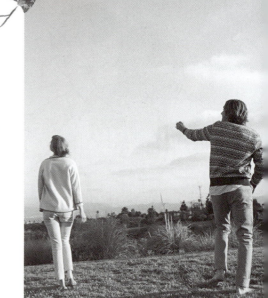

B 🎧 21 Listen to the conversations. Write the weather words you hear.

Conversation 1: _____

Conversation 2: _____

Conversation 3: _____

Conversation 4: _____

C Choose the correct option to complete the sentences.

1 Look at the snow / snowy outside!
2 It isn't rain / raining right now.
3 It will be storm / stormy tomorrow.
4 Listen to the wind / windy!
5 Does it rain / rainy a lot in your country?
6 It's very cloud / cloudy today.

2 GRAMMAR: *may*, *might*, and *will* for future possibility

A Choose the correct option to complete the sentences.

1 I'm sure you may / will have a good time at the concert.
2 I'm not sure, but I may / will be home early tonight.
3 We might / will definitely meet again.
4 They might / will go on vacation this year, but they haven't planned it yet.
5 Are you sure it may / will rain tomorrow?
6 We don't know yet, but it might / will be very cold tonight.

B There is one mistake in each sentence. Find and correct it.

1 We might to go swimming this weekend.
   _____

2 I'm sure it willn't rain today.
   _____

3 We may to get a lot of snow this winter.
   _____

4 I may definitely go to the beach next weekend.
   _____

5 They not might go on vacation this year.
   _____

6 It will be probably sunny tomorrow.
   _____

C Make sentences about the pictures. Use *may*, *might*, or *will*. More than one answer is possible.

1   a)   not find a new job (*not sure*)
    b)   get some good advice (*sure*)

2   a)   go into the store (*sure*)
    b)   buy a new dress (*not sure*)

3   a)   not finish her work today (*sure*)
    b)   be very tired when she goes home (*not sure*)

1   a)   *He may/might not find a new job.*   2   a)   _____
    b)   _____   b)   _____
3   a)   _____
    b)   _____

3 SPEAKING: interrupting

A Write the words in the correct order to make ways of interrupting.

1   me / excuse / for / I / interrupt / you / a / can / second / ?
    Excuse me, _____
2   ask / question / quick / can / I / a / me / excuse / ?
    _____
3   interrupt / sorry / what / the / homework / was / to / but / ?
    _____

B 🎧 22 Listen to the conversations. Use key words to complete the table.

	What is the topic of the main conversation?	Reason for interrupting
Conversation 1		
Conversation 2		
Conversation 3		

4 VOCABULARY: the natural world

A Label the map with the names of the natural features in the box.

field   forest   hill   island   lake   mountain   river   sea

B Complete the descriptions with words from Exercise A.
1. Australia is the largest _Island_ in the world.
2. Baikal is a large _Lake_ in central Russia.
3. Everest is the highest _mountain_ in the Himalayas.
4. The Mediterranean is the _sea_ between Europe and North Africa.
5. The Nile is a _river_ that runs through Egypt.
6. The Amazon is a large tropical _forest_ in South America.

(1) Forest
(2) Hill
(3) Mountain
(4) Sea
(5) Lake
(6) River
(7) Island
(8) Field

5 READING: understanding meaning from context

A Quickly read this article, ignoring any words or phrases you don't know. Then read the sentences and circle T (true) or F (false).

The Amazon Rain forest

The Amazon Rain forest is located in South America near the equator. The forest covers several countries including Brazil, Peru, and Colombia. It is the largest rain forest in the world and is home to millions of different animal and insect species, as well as over 40,000 plant species. These include many **unknown** plants and animals that may be useful in research for new medicines.

Some environmentalists predict that the rain forest may not **survive** for much longer. The main problem is **deforestation**. Farmers are cutting down trees to make farms and fields. People are also cutting down trees to build homes. Global warming is a problem, too. Some experts suggest that a rise in world temperatures might **destroy** around 75% of the Amazon Rain forest. If this happens, many plants and animals will lose their natural **habitat,** and we will lose an important part of our planet's ecosystem.

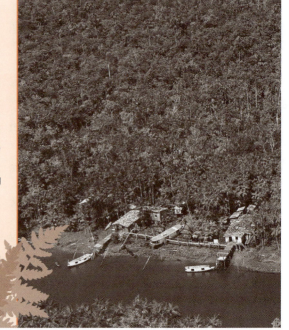

1. The Amazon Rain forest is larger than other forests.   **T** / F
2. Millions of animals live in the Amazon Rain forest.   **T** / F
3. Farms help to protect the rain forest.   T / **F**
4. Climate change will affect the Amazon Rain forest.   **T** / F

B Read the article again and look at the words in bold. Look at the context carefully and choose the correct meaning.

1. unknown — a) natural — b) new
2. survive — a) continue to live — b) get bigger
3. deforestation — a) losing trees — b) planting trees
4. destroy — a) improve — b) kill
5. habitat — a) home — b) climate

6 GRAMMAR: *will* and *going to*

A Match the sentences 1–6 to the correct description a–c.

1. [c] I'll take you on a trip to the mountains.
2. [ ] I'm going to help clean up the beach this weekend.
3. [ ] Climate change will continue to cause floods.
4. [ ] We're going to hike in the forest next week.
5. [ ] Many regions are going to have a lot of rain this year.
6. [ ] I'll try to do more to stop climate change.

a) make a prediction about the future
b) talk about future plans and intentions
c) make spontaneous offers and decisions

B How do you think climate change will affect us in the future? Complete the sentences with *will* or *won't*.

1. Pollution _____ get worse.
2. The earth's climate _____ get warmer.
3. The global population _____ increase.
4. Some countries _____ have enough food.
5. Some animal species _____ survive.
6. Icebergs _____ melt.

C 🎧 23 Complete the conversations with the correct form of *will* or *going to* and the verb in parentheses. Then listen and check your answers.

Conversation 1

A: What (1) _____ you _____ (do) to help the environment?
B: I (2) _____ (not drive) my car when I can use public transportation. What about you?
A: We (3) _____ (save) electricity by using solar panels on our house.
B: That's a good idea! (4) _____ there _____ (be) enough sunshine?
A: Well, there (5) _____ (not be) as much sunshine in the winter, but there should be enough daylight.

Conversation 2

A: I (6) _____ (join) this new climate change organization.
B: Really? What (7) _____ they _____ (do) to stop climate change?
A: They (8) _____ (make) simple changes. For example, I (9) _____ (ride) my bike to work, and I (10) _____ (not use) plastic bags.
B: That's a good idea! Maybe I (11) _____ (do) that, too!

Listen and write

A Look at the pictures. In which place would you like to live?

B 🎧 24 Listen to three people talking about their ideal place to live. Match each person to the correct picture in Exercise A.

Person 1: _cold   2_
Person 2: _sunny 3_
Person 3: _clody + wel 1_

C Listen again and take notes.

	1	2	3
Country / City	Greece	Italy, Tuscany	New York city Manhattan
Natural features / Climate	warm an sunny	hot + warm	
Advantages	beach beauty sea clair blue	large garden lot of flowers	public transportation
Disadvantages	cate cach fish	lonely	noisy + expensive
Lifestyle activities	very relaxed fishing		enjoy eating out every day

D What is your ideal place to live? Choose one place in the world and describe it. Make notes.

Kind of place (e.g., town, village, island, etc.)	Iprene
Natural features / Climate	very cold
Advantages / Disadvantages	calm nature / less activites shoping
Lifestyle activities	sport, running

Over to You

E ✏️ Use your notes from Exercise D to write a paragraph in your notebook about your ideal place to live and explain why.

WRITING TUTOR

My ideal place to live is …
My dream home is in/on/near a …
Some people might want to live in/on/near a … , but I'm going to live in/on/near a …

DOWN TIME

A Choose the one that doesn't belong.
1 island   hill   field   snow
2 rain   wind   island   fog
3 lake   mountain   sea   river
4 sunny   rain   snow   hail
5 windy   weather   rainy   foggy

B Look at the clues and complete the crossword.

1 across: island
3 across: forest
6 across: mountain
7 across: cloudy
2 down: sunny
4 down: sunny
5 down: windy
8 down: lake

Our planet   UNIT 9   57

UNIT 10   PARTY ANIMALS

1 VOCABULARY: parties

A Complete the missing words.

1. h____ a conversation

2. give a _____

3. d_____ the house

4. Welcome the g_____

5. bring some s_____

6. p_____ music

B Complete the paragraph with words in the box.

| conversation | decorated | gift | guests | invited | made | music | snacks |

Last Saturday, we had a party for my grandfather's 70th birthday. We **(1)** _____ over 40 **(2)** _____. I prepared the **(3)** _____ and the drinks. My sister **(4)** _____ a delicious cake. It had candles on it. We **(5)** _____ the living room with balloons and paper chains. My sister's husband brought some **(6)** _____ and his guitar. We all sang Happy Birthday and gave Grandpa our **(7)** _____—a large photograph of the whole family. Everyone danced and talked until midnight. I had an interesting **(8)** _____ with some friends about movies and music. Grandpa said the party was awesome!

2 GRAMMAR: infinitives of purpose

A Last weekend, Marisa went to Mexico for a wedding. Complete the list of her preparations for the trip with phrases in the box and the word *to*.

| book a room   buy a new dress   buy some new shoes |
| get some money   pack her bag   reserve a flight   rest |

1. First, she called a hotel _____.
2. Then she went to the airline website _____.
3. Next, she went to the bank _____.
4. After that, she went to a clothes store _____.
5. Then she went to a shoe store _____.
6. Finally, she went home _____ and _____.

WATCH OUT!

✗ She went to Mexico for to see her friend.

✓ _____

B Complete the sentences with *in order to* or *in order not to* and the correct verb in the box.

disturb   help   increase   let   make   take

Rules for parties in the dorm social room

1 You can move furniture out of the living room _____ space for dancing.
2 You can put signs outside _____ guests find their way.
3 Please park cars on the side streets _____ up all the parking spaces.
4 You can open the back windows _____ in fresh air.
5 You should play music quietly _____ other students.
6 Please clear away all the trash _____ more work for the cleaning staff.

3 VOCABULARY: adjectives for describing events

A Choose the correct word to complete the sentences.
1 There were so many people. It was very crowded / empty.
2 I really enjoyed the quiet music. The atmosphere was very lively / relaxed.
3 I didn't like the food. It was great / awful.
4 A lot of people were dancing. It was very lively / relaxed.
5 The music was too loud / soft. I couldn't hear it at all.
6 I had a great time. It was really awful / fun.

B Choose words in the box to describe the two pictures.

lively   loud   relaxed   soft

Atmosphere: _____   Atmosphere: _____
Music: _____   Music: _____

Party animals   UNIT 10   59

4 WRITING: topic sentences

A Choose the best topic sentence for this paragraph.
a) There are many reasons to have a party.
b) Organizing a party can be very stressful.
c) Parties are a good way to meet people.

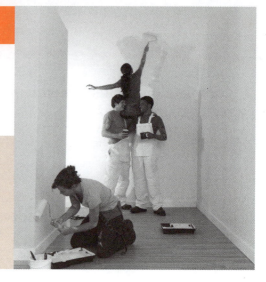

Many people have a party to celebrate their birthday. It's also popular to have parties when you get engaged or married. In some countries, people like to have a housewarming party to celebrate moving into a new home. A recent trend is the "painting party" where you invite friends over to paint the walls of your new home. It's fun and a great way to get some help with fixing up your new home.

B Match the topic sentences to the correct paragraph.
a) It's important to create a good atmosphere.
b) It's a good idea to prepare the food well in advance.
c) A good host makes every guest feel welcome.

TOP TIPS Party Etiquette

1 _____ c _____ When they arrive, go to the door to greet them. Shake their hands and make them feel that you are pleased to see them. Then introduce them to some of the other guests. Think of a topic they have in common and get them talking to each other before you move on. If they feel welcome, everyone will be more relaxed and ready to have a good time.

2 _____ You can use lighting to create a different mood, or move your furniture around to create more space. Decorate your room and play some music in the background because it will help people to relax. Soft music will encourage good conversations and people will not have to shout. Put chairs around the room, but not too many. You want people to move around and not stay sitting in one place.

3 _____ Make a list of all the snacks and drinks you need, and if appropriate, ask your guests to bring something to eat and drink. Make sure you have food for vegetarians and those who are allergic to nuts or milk. Provide a variety of drinks. Make sure you have plenty of extra bread or crackers in case you run out of food at the end of the party.

5 LISTENING: understanding agreement and disagreement

A Write the expressions in the correct place in the table.

I completely agree.   I don't agree.   I don't think that's right   I'm not sure I agree.
That's not true.   Yes, that's right.   Yes, that's true.   You're absolutely right.

Strongly agree	Agree	Disagree	Strongly disagree

B 🎧 **25** Listen to the conversations and decide if the two people agree or disagree.

1. agree / disagree
2. agree / disagree
3. agree / disagree

C Listen again. Which three phrases are in the conversations? Write the number of the conversation.

- ☐ I completely agree.
- ☐ I don't agree.
- ☐ I'm not sure I agree.
- ☐ That's not true.
- ☐ Yes, that's right.
- ☐ Yes, that's true.
- ☐ You're absolutely right.
- ☐ I don't think that's right.

6 GRAMMAR: review of future forms

A Match sentences 1–6 to their meanings a–f.

1. The party starts at nine tonight.
2. We're renting a large hall for the party.
3. The weather will be fine.
4. We're going to invite all our friends.
5. I'll help you clean up after the party.
6. I'm going to have a party next week.

a) future arrangement
b) intention
c) future prediction
d) future plan
e) spontaneous decision
f) scheduled event

B Choose the correct option.

1. **A:** I have / am having a party on Saturday. Can you come?
   B: Sure! I'll / I'm going to come over about seven, OK?
2. **A:** What are you going to / will you cook for the guests?
   B: We're having / We'll have a barbecue. It's all prepared.
3. **A:** We're going / We'll go on vacation tomorrow.
   B: Really? Where will you / are you going to go?
4. **A:** Let's go! The train is leaving / leaves at six.
   B: OK. It won't take / It's not taking long to get there.
5. **A:** What do you do / are you doing tonight?
   B: I'm going to / I'll watch a movie on TV.

WATCH OUT!

✗ Do you stay at home tonight?
✓ _____

C Complete the email with the correct future form of the verb in parentheses.

Dear Carrie,
Thanks so much for your email. I'm very excited to hear about your housewarming party! What time **(1)** _____ it _____ (start)? What **(2)** _____ you _____ (wear)? I think I **(3)** _____ (wear) my green silk dress. Hopefully, we **(4)** _____ (have) some nice weather and we can sit outside. What kind of food **(5)** _____ you _____ (make)? **(6)** I _____ (bring) some cookies and some salad—is that OK? I'm sorry that Mark **(7)** _____ (come). He **(8)** _____ (work)! He **(9)** _____ (go) to an important conference on Monday. Could I ask my neighbor Paula to come instead? I'm sure she **(10)** _____ (be) thrilled!
See you soon!
Love, Tina

Read and write

A Read the letters and check the party you would rather go to.

☐

Hi Lucy!

I'm planning a birthday party for next week. Can you come? It's going to be at my house, and I'm going to invite about 20 people. It starts at 9 p.m. I want to have a horror movie theme, so you could dress up as Dracula or a vampire if you want! We're going to decorate the house with horror movie posters, and play loud, scary music. Could you think of some strange and unusual foods for us to eat?

Angie

☐

Hi Brendan!

We're having a housewarming party on Saturday. Would you like to come? We're inviting just a few friends, and our new neighbor is going to play a few songs on his guitar, so it'll be a nice, relaxed atmosphere with some fantastic live music. Melissa is making a salad, and Jeff is bringing the dessert. Could you bring some lemonade and orange juice? I can come and pick you up at your house if you want. Let me know.

Paul

B Answer the questionnaire about your ideal party.

Your Ideal Birthday Party Use this questionnaire to plan your party.

1. Where will the party be?
   ☐ in your home   ☐ in a restaurant   other: _____
2. What time will the party start?
   ☐ 3 p.m.   ☐ 7 p.m.   other: _____
3. What kind of food will you have?
   ☐ snacks   ☐ desserts   ☐ sandwiches   other: _____
4. What kind of music will you have?
   ☐ loud   ☐ soft   other: _____
5. What will you ask your guests to bring?
   ☐ food   ☐ drinks   other: _____
6. What kind of theme will you have (e.g., horror movie theme)?
   _____
7. How will you decorate the party space?
   _____

Over to You

C ✎ Write a letter to a friend in your notebook. Invite your friend to the party and describe what it will be like. Use the letters in Exercise A and the information from the questionnaire in Exercise B to help you.

DOWN TIME

A Match the antonyms (words with the opposite meaning).

empty
old
large
tall
quiet
small
short
noisy
new
relaxing
crowded
stressful

B Match the synonyms (words with the same meaning).

boring
awful
enormous
huge
dull
lively
tiny
noisy
loud
small
exciting
terrible

C Read the clues. What's the mystery message?

1. The antonym of *soft*, first letter. _____
2. The synonym of *awful*, second letter. _____
3. The antonym of *crowded*, fourth letter. _____
4. Something you eat at a party, first letter. _____
5. The antonym of *sad*, first letter. _____
6. The antonym of *big*, third letter. _____
7. Exciting and active, third letter. _____
8. The synonym of *big*, last letter. _____
9. The antonym of *fantastic*, third letter. _____
10. People who go to a party, second letter. _____
11. The antonym of *quiet*, first letter. _____

Mystery message: __ __ __ ' __ __ __ __ __ __ __ __ !
                     1   2   3   4   5   6   7   8   9   10   11

UNIT 11 INNOVATE!

1 VOCABULARY: materials

A Match the materials in the box to the products.

| ceramic cotton glass metal nylon plastic rubber wood |

1
2
3
4
5
6
7
8

B What materials are these products made of? More than one answer may be possible.

1 credit card _____
2 bench _____
3 shopping bag _____
4 dress _____
5 sunglasses _____
6 vase _____

2 GRAMMAR: simple present passive

A Read the sentences. Are they A (active) or P (passive)?

1 These gloves are made of cotton. ____
2 We use silk and cotton to make these rugs. ____
3 They make ceramic chips in this factory. ____
4 Cotton is produced in India. ____
5 Picnic plates are made of plastic or paper. ____
6 We use nylon string for the parachutes. ____

WATCH OUT!

✗ The table is make of wood.

✓ _____

64

B Complete the sentences using the simple present passive of the verbs in parentheses.

1. This software *is sold* (sell) on the internet.
2. This product _____ (manufacture) in South Korea.
3. These screens _____ (make) from plastic.
4. Old cell phones _____ (not recycle).
5. _____ cars _____ (produce) in Mexico?
6. This camera _____ (use) to make videos.

C There is one mistake in each sentence. Find and correct it.

1. Plastic and glass are not recycle in my country.
2. Solar energy used to generate electricity.
3. Computers is used to control the temperature.
4. Cell phones are selled in electronics stores.
5. This app can be download onto your smartphone.

3 READING: understanding meaning from context

A Read this page from a technology website. Choose a suitable title for the text.

a) Many ways to make phone calls.
b) Smartphones of tomorrow.
c) How to use your phone.

HOME GUIDES FEATURES FORUMS SHOP REVIEWS NEWS PODCASTS

These days, smartphones do so much more than cell phones of the past. We already use them in **multiple** different ways: to make phone calls and to send text messages, to access the internet, send emails, and check the weather, the traffic, the train times—in fact, any kind of information is at our fingertips. So how can smartphones become even better?

One way in which smartphones are going to **improve** is that they will be able to **interact** with the environment. For example, if you visit a new place, you can hold up your phone, take a picture of the place, and your phone will tell you all kinds of information about where you are and what you can do there.

Another **development** will be 3D imaging. We will not only see our friends' faces on the screen, their image will pop out, and you'll see their whole body, and they'll move around just like a real person, but much smaller. This will enhance and improve the way we interact with other people via our phones.

Finally, when you want your phone to do something, you won't need to type anything. You can just speak to the phone, and the phone will **carry out** your instructions.

B Read the text again and look at the words in bold. Look at the context carefully and choose the correct meaning.

1	multiple	a)	a few	b)	many	c) interesting
2	improve	a)	add	b)	invent	c) become better
3	interact	a)	respond to	b)	change	c) speak to
4	development	a)	improvement	b)	equipment	c) statement
5	carry out	a)	do	b)	tell	c) create

Innovate! UNIT 11 65

4 GRAMMAR: simple past passive

A Look at the pictures. Complete the sentences about each one using the simple past passive of the verbs in parentheses.

1 The first photograph _____ in 1826. (*take*)

2 The first phone call _____ in 1876. (*make*)

3 The first computer mouse _____ in 1963. (*invent*)

4 The first digital cameras _____ in 1991. (*develop*)

5 The first camera phones _____ in Japan in 2001. (*sell*)

B Write the questions and sentences using the simple past passive. Use *by* if necessary.

1 When / the World Wide Web / create ?

Tim Berners-Lee / 1989

2 When / the first iPhones® / produce ?

2007

3 When / the Apple® logo / design ?

Rob Janoff / 1977

4 When / the computer mouse / invent ?

Douglas Engelbart / 1963

5 VOCABULARY: technology

A Complete the sentences with words in the box.

add   back up   click   install   log on   print out   right-click   type in

1. You need to _____ your files regularly if you don't want to lose them.
2. Just _____ on the browser icon and the internet will open up on your desktop.
3. Why don't you _____ this antivirus program on your computer?
4. I want to _____ to my email account, but I can't remember my password.
5. If you _____ your username and password, you can see your account details.
6. You can _____ on the file name and select "send" to save the file on your flash drive.
7. When your transaction is complete, you can _____ this message for your files.
8. Some people _____ all their friends' names to their social-network page.

B Complete the text with words from Exercise A.

MAGIC FILE ORGANIZER:
Save time and money!

Stressed out with documents you can't find? Need help with organizing your files more efficiently? Use our website! It's easy. Just **(1)** _____ with your username and password. Then **(2)** _____ the name of your file in the search box. If you want to **(3)** _____ one of our programs, **(4)** _____ on the icon and select "download." If you want to **(5)** _____ a document, just **(6)** _____ on the printer icon at the top of the page. Worried about losing your files when your computer crashes? Just **(7)** _____ your files on our memory cloud! Tell your friends! Why not **(8)** _____ us to your social-network page?

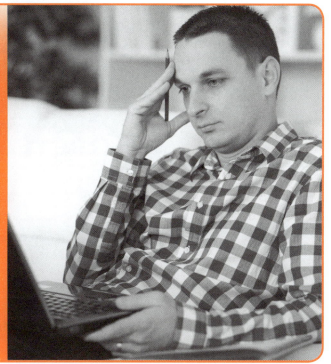

6 SPEAKING: expressing uncertainty

A 🎧 26 Listen to the conversations. What kind of gadget or device is each person trying to use?

1. _____
2. _____
3. _____
4. _____

B Listen again. Which phrases for expressing uncertainty do you hear? Write the number of the conversation.

☐ I guess so.   ☐ I'm not sure.   ☐ I suppose so.
☐ I think …   ☐ Maybe …   ☐ … probably …

Innovate!   UNIT 11   67

Listen and write

A 🎧 27 Listen to an interview with Tracy talking about a gadget she can't live without. Choose T (true) or F (false) or DS (doesn't say).

1 She doesn't like going out without her phone. T / F / DS
2 She uses her smartphone mainly for work. T / F / DS
3 She uses it to communicate with friends. T / F / DS
4 She doesn't use it to look up information. T / F / DS
5 She enjoys playing games on it. T / F / DS
6 She often listens to music on it. T / F / DS

B Listen again and write six ways of using a smartphone mentioned by Tracy.

1 to keep _____
2 to get _____
3 to look up _____
4 to check _____
5 to store her _____
6 to listen to _____

Why do you think Tracy likes her smartphone? _____

C Think of a gadget you can't live without. Make notes in the table below.

Name of gadget	What can it be used for?	Why do you like it?

Over to You

D ✏️ Use your notes from Exercise C to write a paragraph in your notebook about your favorite gadget.

WRITING TUTOR

Something I can't live without is my …
The most important gadget for me is my …
It's impossible for me to go anywhere without my …

DOWN TIME

A Put the pieces together to make six gadgets. Write the letters of the pieces in the table. Then write the names of the gadgets next to the letters.

	Puzzle piece	Name of gadget
1		
2		
3		
4		
5		
6		

B Write the name of each type of material. Then unscramble the shaded letters to find the name of a gadget.

Mystery gadget: _ _ _ _ _ _

UNIT 12 ACROSS THE GENERATIONS

1 VOCABULARY: describing relationships

A Match the phrases to their definitions.

1 admire
2 get along with
3 have arguments
4 make up
5 share the same values
6 go through

a) to experience
b) to agree about the important things in life
c) to disagree
d) to be friends with someone
e) to become friendly again after an argument
f) to respect or look up to someone

B 🎧 28 Complete the sentences with words from Exercise A. Then listen and check your answers.

The person I **(1)** _____ most in my family is my mother. She works really hard to make sure our home is comfortable and clean, and she always makes delicious food for us. We don't really appreciate her enough.
I have two sisters and one brother. We **(2)** _____ from time to time, but we usually **(3)** _____ again soon after. I'd say I **(4)** _____ all of them, especially with my brother. He's my best friend.
I think that the younger generation often has different opinions than their parents.
They don't always **(5)** _____, but I think that's something we all **(6)** _____ as we grow up.

2 GRAMMAR: zero and first conditionals

A Decide if the sentence is in the zero conditional or first conditional.

1 If you don't make mistakes, you won't learn anything.
  a) zero conditional   b) first conditional
2 You'll learn a lot if you listen to your parents.
  a) zero conditional   b) first conditional
3 Our parents get upset if we don't do our homework.
  a) zero conditional   b) first conditional
4 If parents are too strict, their children won't obey them.
  a) zero conditional   b) first conditional
5 If I need advice, I ask my parents first.
  a) zero conditional   b) first conditional
6 If my friend has a problem, I try to help him or her.
  a) zero conditional   b) first conditional

WATCH OUT!

✗ If you will help me, I help you.
✓

B Choose the correct options to complete the sentences.

Zero conditionals
1. If we *have* / *will have* a fight, we *try* / *will try* to make up soon after.
2. My parents *get* / *will get* upset if I *don't* / *won't* obey them.
3. If I *don't* / *won't* understand a question, I usually *ask* / *will ask* my teacher.
4. You *find* / *will find* a solution more easily if you *talk* / *will talk* about your problems.

First conditionals
5. If you *give* / *will give* him a chance, I think you *get* / *will get* along well.
6. I *try* / *will try* to help you with your homework if you *call* / *will call* me later.
7. If he *doesn't* / *won't* come home by 10 p.m., he *doesn't* / *won't* go out again this month.
8. We *won't be* / *aren't* tired tomorrow if we *go* / *will go* to sleep early tonight.

C There is one mistake in each sentence. Find and correct it.
1. If I won't have breakfast, I can't concentrate. _____
2. You will feel tired if you won't get enough sleep. _____
3. We won't get to school on time if we won't leave now. _____
4. Our parents get worried if we not home on time. _____

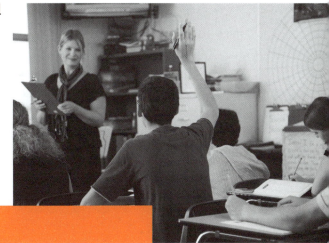

3 VOCABULARY: values

A Match the sentences to the values they express.
1. Having a permanent job with a good salary is important to me.
2. I hate having to borrow money or ask for help.
3. I love to discover new places and have new experiences.
4. It's important to share my ideas through art, writing, or music.
5. I want to be famous and important.
6. I try to give time to people who need help.

a) express creativity
b) help my community
c) be independent
d) have security
e) find adventure
f) have status

B Complete the blog entries with words in the box.

> hard work   have power   having good friendships   help my community   job satisfaction   job security

What values are most important to you in your life?

My job is the most important thing for me. I don't mean a job that pays a lot of money. **(1)** _____ isn't the main thing, but a job that I believe in and that gives me **(2)** _____ .

In addition to work and family, I think it's important to **(4)** _____ . I work as a volunteer in a hospital, and it makes me feel good to help other people. People really appreciate my help.

I think that **(3)** _____ is the most important thing. I like to spend time with people I love and that takes time and energy.

My goal is to **(5)** _____ and be successful. And **(6)** _____ is the only way to get success. If you're lazy, you won't get anywhere.

4 LISTENING: understanding agreement and disagreement

A 🎧 29 Listen to the conversation. Do the speakers generally agree or disagree?

B Listen again. Which statements do both speakers agree about and which do they disagree about?

1 People are more willing to change their jobs these days. agree / disagree
2 People are unhappy if they don't get promoted quickly. agree / disagree
3 Work isn't important to people these days. agree / disagree
4 People have a better balance of work and free time these days. agree / disagree

C Listen again. Number these expressions in the order that you hear them.

☐ Actually, I think you're right.
☐ I'm not sure about that.
☐ Exactly.
☐ Yes, that's true.
☐ Well, I think …
☐ I think you're forgetting that …

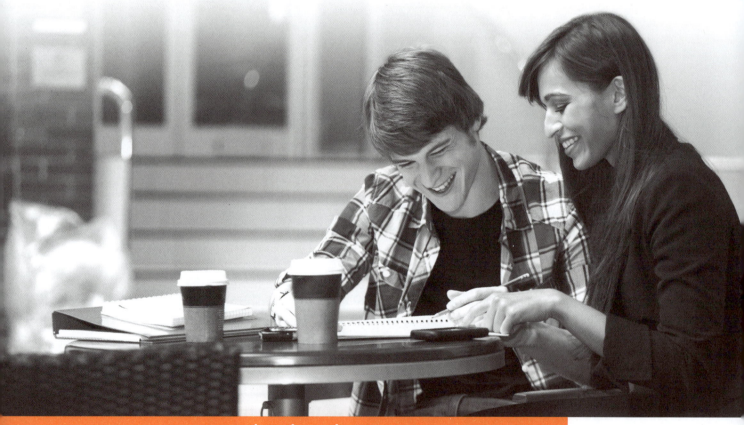

5 GRAMMAR: second conditional

A Choose the correct option.

1 If I had / have enough money, I'd buy a bigger house and a new car.
2 Will / Would you change your job if they offered you more money?
3 If I worked at home, I could / can spend more time with my family.
4 I won't / wouldn't be happy if I lived away from home.
5 What would / will you do if you had a year off?
6 If you didn't work so hard, you won't / wouldn't feel so tired.
7 I'm sure you would / will be happier if you had more free time.
8 What would you do if you are / were in my shoes?

B Read each question and choose one option. Then write a sentence to say what you would do. Use the second conditional.

1   You suddenly lose your job.
    a) look for a new job right away
    b) take a year off and travel
    c) decide to do something new
       If _____ .

2   You find $100 in a wallet on the bus.
    a) tell the bus driver
    b) take it to the police
    c) take it home
       If _____ .

3   You see a small child crying in the supermarket.
    a) call the store manager
    b) sit down and talk to the child
    c) not do anything
       If _____ .

4   You have an argument with your brother or sister.
    a) apologize and make up
    b) cry and feel miserable
    c) not say anything
       If _____ .

6 WRITING: paragraphs

A Read the topic sentence for a paragraph. Decide which five sentences are appropriate supporting sentences for the topic. Then number them in the best order.

Topic sentence: Many young people take a year off before they start college.
- [ ] It is an opportunity to get real-life experience.
- [ ] It is difficult to live at home when you're at college.
- [ ] They can think carefully about what they want to study at college.
- [ ] They can travel to other countries, or find a job.
- [ ] It can be a lot of fun.
- [ ] It helps young people develop confidence and maturity.

B Write the paragraph in your notebook. Use these words to introduce the supporting details.
- For example,
- Also,
- In addition,
- Finally,

C 🎧 30 Listen to one possible answer.

Across the generations   UNIT 12   73

Read and write

A Read Xiang's essay about personal values and circle T (true) or F (false).

My personal values

Children learn about values within their family. These values can be very strong and last a lifetime. My parents taught my brother, my sister, and me that it is important to have our own opinions, and to respect other people's opinions, too. For example, whenever I had an argument with my brother or sister, our parents asked us to explain what the argument was about and why we disagreed. This way, we learned to listen to each other. If people listen to each other, they can learn to respect different opinions and values.

I also learned that it is important to work hard. We had to do jobs around the house, such as washing the dishes, cleaning our rooms, or watering the plants in the garden to earn our allowance. When we were older, we had part-time jobs to earn money to buy things we wanted like comics or CDs. If you have to work for your money, you are more careful about how to spend it.

I admire my parents because they taught us important values. In the future, if I have children, I'll try to help them develop their identity and to be independent. If I listen to their opinions and show that we can love and respect each other, it will give them a good example to follow in their lives.

1 Xiang's parents taught her to express her opinions.   T / F
2 She sometimes disagreed with her brother and sister.   T / F
3 She never had to do chores for her allowance.   T / F
4 She always had a lot of money as a child.   T / F
5 She spent more money than she had.   T / F
6 She wants her children to be independent.   T / F

> Notice how Xiang introduces a personal value. Then she gives an example. Then she describes what she learned.

B Complete the chart with your own ideas.

Personal values	Examples	If you become a parent, how will you share these values with your children?
1. _____	1. _____	1. _____
2. _____	2. _____	2. _____

Over to You

C ✏ Use your notes in Exercise B to write a paragraph in your notebook about your personal values.

WRITING TUTOR

My parents taught me …
I also learned from my parents that …
For example, …
This way …
If …, then you …

DOWN TIME

A Read the clues. Complete the crossword.

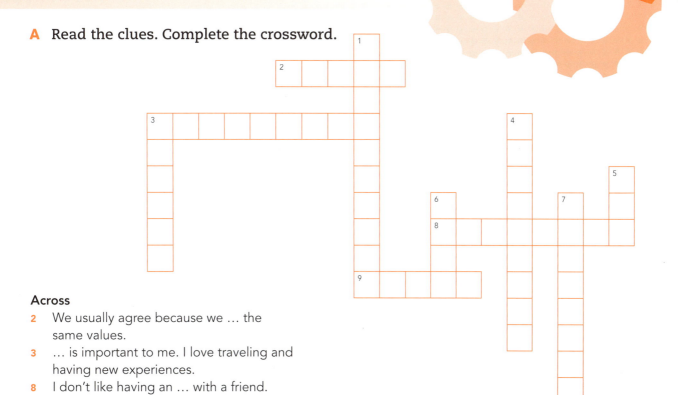

Across
2 We usually agree because we … the same values.
3 … is important to me. I love traveling and having new experiences.
8 I don't like having an … with a friend.
9 Politicians usually have a lot of …

Down
1 I enjoy spending time with my friends. … is important to me.
3 I … my brother because he is very creative.
4 I like to help others in my … so I do a lot of charity work.
5 I try to … along with everyone in my family and we have a good time together.
6 Sometimes we disagree, but we … up soon after.
7 I want a job that's safe and has a lot of …

B Match the parts of the words in the boxes to find seven words for values in our lives. Then write them in order of importance for you.

FRI	VE	LY
INDE	ER	
MON	EY	ENCE
POW	UR	
SEC	PEND	HIP
FA	ENDS	
LO	MI	ITY

1 _____   4 _____   7 _____
2 _____   5 _____
3 _____   6 _____

Across the generations   **UNIT 12**   **75**

Audio script

UNIT 7
Track 16
- **A:** Welcome to our "Guess the Food" contest! Four volunteers from the audience are going to wear a blindfold and taste these foods without seeing or smelling them. Can they guess what they're eating? We start with volunteer number one.
- **B:** Mmm … I'm eating this with a spoon. It's a little greasy, but it's also crunchy, salty, and sweet at the same time. Oh, it tastes like nuts. I think I know exactly what it is. It's … peanut butter!
- **A:** Good job! That's the correct answer! Now volunteer number two.
- **C:** This is interesting, OK, I'm eating this with a fork. It's creamy and sweet. Definitely sweet with a sort of lemony flavor, oh, and it has a crunchy cookie-type of base at the bottom—mmm, delicious! I think it's … cheesecake.
- **A:** Yes, that's right! It was lemon cheesecake. Congratulations! And now volunteer number three.
- **D:** Let's see, I'm holding a piece of this food in my fingers. It's … it's very juicy … ahhh, it's really sour! That's … a lemon.
- **A:** Sorry! Are you OK? But you did a good job. And you were right. This is a lemon! And now our last volunteer, number four.
- **E:** It's soft. I'm eating this with a fork, but it's very salty … oh, yes, and very, very hot and spicy … oh, it's burning my mouth! I recognize this. It's fried beans with chili peppers.
- **A:** Spicy! That's right! Good job and thank you to all of our volunteers today!

Track 17
- **A:** Thanks so much for helping me with the picnic today, Yuki.
- **B:** No problem! I'm happy to help. I hope I got enough food at the supermarket.
- **A:** OK, let's check the list and see. How many bags of potato chips did you get?
- **B:** Ten, and six packages of cookies, too.
- **A:** That's great. And how many cans of soda?
- **B:** Twelve—one for each of us. And two large bottles of water.
- **A:** Perfect! And I already have a large bottle of orange juice. Did you get any bread?
- **B:** Yes, I bought two loaves of bread, three jars of peanut butter, and three jars of jam.
- **A:** Wonderful! I think that will be enough for everyone!
- **B:** There's only one problem. I'm on a diet, and I can't eat any of this food. So I brought some apples for *my* lunch!

Track 18
1. While I was in Australia, I visited a restaurant that served crocodile stew. The crocodile meat was extremely tough and not that tasty. In fact, it was too difficult to chew, and I gave up halfway through.
2. In Sweden they eat this strange kind of pickled herring. It's kept in a wooden barrel for a year. You eat it with potatoes, a little onion, and a few tomatoes. It's usually served on thin, hard bread. It tastes delicious, kind of sour and sweet at the same time—but the smell is disgusting!
3. The most unusual food I have ever tasted is a peanut butter and jam sandwich. I can't believe people eat that for lunch in the U.S.A. Why would you put salty food and sweet food together like that? It's not healthy enough, and it tastes really strange.

UNIT 8
Track 19
- **A:** Have Mike and Rachel broken up? I haven't seen them together recently.
- **B:** Yes, Mike's going out with Julianna now. I think they just got engaged.
- **A:** Really? They haven't known each other that long, right?
- **B:** No, they met on a blind date about a month ago. The next day, he asked her out again, and the rest is history.
- **A:** That's great news! I hope they'll be happy!

Track 20
The Eastern Brown Pelican is a brownish-gray bird with a large pouch under its beak. Pelicans live in Florida in very large numbers in the bird preservation area known as Pelican Island.

Pelicans reproduce once a year, laying two to three eggs at a time. The male and female pelicans work together to make the nest and incubate the eggs. The males collect the building material and the females build the nest. The nests are on the ground. They incubate the eggs for 28 to 30 days.

It is amazing that Pelican chicks can learn to communicate with their parents while they are still inside the egg. Pelican chicks make sounds from inside the egg when they are too hot or cold!

Both parents feed and care for their young. They take turns catching fish during the day, and bring the fish back to the nest, carrying it in their beaks. The young pelicans dip their beaks into the parents' beaks to get the fish. Baby pelicans often learn to swim before they learn to fly.

UNIT 9
Track 21
1.
   - **A:** Hi, Dale. How's the weather in Boston today? Is it cold?
   - **B:** Yes, it's very, very cold! We've had about two feet of snow since yesterday, and we spent all this morning shoveling the sidewalk and trying to dig our car out! The kids love it—they made an amazing snowman!
2.
   - **A:** Oh, hi, Jackie. Where are you?
   - **B:** We're on the beach! It's a gorgeous sunny day here in Miami—not a cloud in the sky, and the temperature is wonderful! It's hot, but not too hot—around 80 degrees.
   - **A:** Sounds perfect, I wish I was there!
3.
   - **A:** How's the weather in San Francisco today?
   - **B:** Oh, you know … the usual … it's a cold gray day, very cloudy. I think it's going to rain soon. I wanted to go out for a walk at lunchtime, but it was too wet and too windy.
4.
   - **A:** What's the weather like there today?
   - **B:** Oh, it's kind of nasty, you know. It was very cold overnight, about 30 degrees, and now it's foggy, and visibility is really low. The weather forecast says it's going to get stormy later this afternoon. Not great, really.

Track 22
1.
   - **A:** Could you make copies of these letters, please?
   - **B:** I might not have time before lunch. Is that OK?
   - **C:** Sorry to interrupt. Could I borrow your pen for a moment?
   - **B:** Yes, of course. Here you are.
2.
   - **A:** Do you want to have lunch in the cafeteria?
   - **B:** Yes, I'd like that very much!
   - **C:** Sorry, can I interrupt for a second? Which way is the cafeteria?
   - **B:** Oh, we're going that way. Why don't you come with us?

3 A: Could I get some information about the new courses, please?
   B: Yes, sure. Here's the latest course listing and class timetable. Do you think you might be interested?
   C: Excuse me, can I ask a quick question? Could I have one of those timetables, please?
   B: Yes, of course. Here you go.

Track 23
1 A: What are you going to do to help the environment?
   B: I'm not going to drive my car when I can use public transportation. What about you?
   A: We're going to save electricity by using solar panels on our house.
   B: That's a good idea! Will there be enough sunshine?
   A: Well, there won't be as much sunshine in the winter, but there should be enough daylight.
2 A: I'm going to join this new climate change organization.
   B: Really? What are they going to do to stop climate change?
   A: They're going to make simple changes. For example, I'm going to ride my bike to work, and I'm not going to use plastic bags.
   B: That's a good idea! Maybe I'll do that, too!

Track 24
1 I'm going to live on a small island in Greece. I'll live in a small village near the sea. The weather there is warm and sunny every day. The beach has beautiful white sand. The sea is clear and blue, and the water is warm. I'll have a small house on the beach and a little fishing boat. Every morning, I'll go out and catch fish. In the afternoon, I'll take a nap under a palm tree. My lifestyle will be very relaxed.
2 I'm going to live in a small village in Tuscany in Italy. There are hills and fruit trees all around the area. The summers are hot and the winters are warm, but never cold. I'll live on a farm and grow olive trees. I'll also have a large vegetable garden and a lot of flowers. Some people might say it's a little lonely, but I love peace and quiet, and all my friends will visit me, so it'll be wonderful!
3 I'm going to live in New York City. I'll have a small apartment in Manhattan, not far from all the stores and restaurants. I know it's noisy, and expensive, too. But I won't need a car because public transportation is so good, and there are plenty of good places to eat that aren't at all expensive. I'll go out to the theater and to art exhibitions, and enjoy eating out every day.

UNIT 10

Track 25
1 A: I don't like giving parties at home. It's too much work!
   B: I completely agree! I'd much rather go out to a restaurant or a dance club.
2 A: Do you know that new Italian restaurant on the corner? We went there last week, and it was really expensive.
   B: I'm not sure I agree with you. We went there on Tuesday night, and they had a special offer—two meals for the price of one!
3 A: Have you been to that new music club? It's called Maxine's. We went there on Saturday.
   B: Yes, I have. What did you think of it?
   A: I didn't like it all. It was too loud and very crowded.
   B: You're absolutely right. There's too much noise, and the atmosphere is awful.

UNIT 11

Track 26
1 A: Do you know how to use this printer?
   B: Um … I'm not sure … I think if you press this button here … oops, no, that's not it …
   A: Oh, well, don't worry …
2 A: Can you help me with this laptop?
   B: Sure, what do you need?
   A: I'm just trying to turn it on.
   B: Hmm … let's see … you probably need to press this button here.
3 A: How does this smartphone work? I want to access my messages. Is it this button here?
   B: Um … I guess so … oh, it looks a little different from mine …
   A: I tried this button, but nothing happened.
   B: Oh. I see. Maybe you could try this one …
4 A: Can you show me how to use this coffee maker? Do I press this button first?
   B: Oh, I suppose so … let's take a look. First, you select the type of coffee …
   A: And then the start button?
   B: Yes, that's it!

Track 27
A: What's one gadget you can't live without?
B: Oh, that definitely has to be my smartphone! I can't go anywhere without it!
A: What do you generally use it for?
B: Oh, everything! Well, I suppose mainly to make phone calls and send emails and text messages.
A: So … to keep in touch with your friends?
B: That's right. But I also use it as a calendar, and to check where I'm going, and what I'm supposed to be doing!
A: I see, and what else do you use it for?
B: Well, I use it to get directions if I'm going somewhere new, or I use it to look up times of shows or movies, or check reviews of restaurants … and then I have all my pictures stored on there. So I can send pictures to people or show them my pictures.
A: It saves having to carry stuff around with you.
B: Absolutely! It's small enough to go in my pocket. And then, of course, I listen to music on it. I just snap these headphones in, and that's it—I'm in another world!

UNIT 12

Track 28
The person I admire most in my family is my mother. She works really hard to make sure our home is comfortable and clean, and she always makes delicious food for us. We don't really appreciate her enough.
I have two sisters and one brother. We have arguments from time to time, but we usually make up again soon after. I'd say I get along with all of them, especially with my brother. He's my best friend.
I think that the younger generation often has different opinions than their parents. They don't always share the same values, but I think that's something we all go through as we grow up.

Track 29

A: Do you think people's attitudes and expectations about work are changing these days?

B: Well, I think people are more willing to change their jobs and move to another company, or another city, to find better work. Definitely.

A: Yes, that's true. And I also think that when people start a new job, they expect to learn skills they can transfer to another job later. I see that a lot when graduates apply for their first job. They always ask about training and promotions.

B: Yes, but … I think that then they get dissatisfied if they aren't promoted quickly enough.

A: I'm not sure about that. I think people understand that a promotion is the result of hard work *and* experience. And this takes some time.

B: But that's exactly the problem! People's attitudes about hard work are different these days. I think they're less interested in working hard.

A: Hmm. I think you're forgetting that lifestyles have changed. I'd say people have more outside interests, and they're probably better at keeping a work-life balance. But this doesn't mean that they don't work hard.

B: Actually, I think you're right. In my company, there's a sports and fitness club, and they even have yoga classes. People aren't stuck to their desks all day.

B: Exactly. And then they don't get so stressed about work … that's a very good thing!

Track 30

Many young people take a year off before they start college. It is an opportunity to get real-life experience. For example, they can travel to other countries, or find a job. Also, they can think carefully about what they want to study at college. In addition, it helps young people develop confidence and maturity. Finally, it can be a lot of fun.

Answer key

UNIT 7

Section 1
Exercise A
1 sweet 2 salty 3 sour 4 crunchy

Exercise B
Suggested answers
1 apple: juicy, crunchy, sweet
2 mango: juicy, sweet
3 cheese: salty, creamy
4 mustard: creamy, spicy
5 ginger: crunchy, spicy
6 potato chips: crunchy, salty, spicy
7 grapefruit: sour, juicy
8 ice cream: sweet, creamy

Exercise C
Volunteer 1
Description: greasy, crunchy, salty, sweet
Mystery food: peanut butter
Volunteer 2
Description: creamy, sweet, crunchy
Mystery food: lemon cheesecake
Volunteer 3
Description: juicy, sour
Mystery food: lemon
Volunteer 4
Description: soft, salty, spicy
Mystery food: fried beans with chili peppers

Section 2
Exercise A
1 The dessert is not creamy enough.
2 The sauce is too spicy.
3 The toast is not crunchy enough.
4 The ice cream is too sweet.

Watch out!
This coffee isn't <u>hot enough</u>.

Exercise B
1 This soup is too cold.
2 This sauce is salty enough.
3 These French fries are too greasy.
4 These grapes aren't sweet enough.
5 This orange isn't juicy enough.
6 These vegetables aren't crunchy enough.
7 This lemonade is sweet enough.

Section 3
Exercise A
1 a box of chocolates
2 a bag of potato chips
3 a can of soup
4 a package of rice
5 a jar of mayonnaise
6 a bottle of water

Exercise B
1 c 2 c 3 a 4 c 5 a 6 b

Exercise C
10 bags of potato chips
6 packages of cookies
12 cans of soda
2 bottles of water
2 loaves of bread
3 jars of peanut butter
3 jars of jam

Section 4
Exercise A
1 enough 2 too many 3 too much
4 too much 5 enough 6 too many

Exercise B
1 less, less 2 fewer, less 3 less 4 fewer 5 less

Exercise C
1 much 2 little 3 few 4 more 5 many 6 lot

Watch out!
I don't drink <u>much</u> tea.

Section 5
1 B 2 A 3 D 4 C

Section 6
Exercise A
a popular American social event

Exercise B
1 a 2 a

Exercise C
1 a competition 2 visitors 3 no

Listen and write
Exercise A
Speaker 1: C
Speaker 2: B
Speaker 3: A

Exercise B
1 Australia, tough and not that tasty, no
2 Sweden, sweet and sour, yes
3 the U.S.A., salty and sweet, no

DOWN TIME
Exercise A
1 shrimp 2 pasta 3 turkey 4 steak

Exercise B
1 b 2 a 3 c 4 a 5 c 6 c 7 b 8 c 9 a 10 b

UNIT 8

Section 1
Exercise A
1 B 2 C 3 E 4 A 5 D

Exercise B
1 broken up 2 going out 3 got engaged
4 blind date 5 asked, out

Section 2
Exercise A
1 to see 2 eat 3 cooking 4 to go out
5 to go 6 have 7 to cook 8 watching

Exercise B
1 I would like to go to a party.
2 Would you like to go out for dinner?
3 We would rather not go out tonight.
4 Would you prefer to eat at home?
5 I would prefer not to eat Italian food.
6 Would you rather go to a movie?

Watch out!
I'd rather not <u>see</u> a movie tonight.

Exercise C
1 Would you prefer to go to a movie?
2 Would you prefer to talk in a café?
3 Would you rather meet with a group of friends?
4 Would you rather go dancing?
5 Would you prefer to talk about music?
6 Would you like to have dinner with your parents?

Section 3
Exercise A
1 having—After a preposition
2 Going—Subject
3 dancing, listening—Object
4 talking—After a preposition
5 giving—Object
6 playing—Subject

Exercise B
1 Filling 2 Giving 3 going 4 asking 5 Getting
6 going 7 Chatting 8 dating 9 Meeting 10 making

Watch out!
I really enjoy going to parties.

Exercise C
1 Meeting people at parties is easy.
2 Having dinner with friends is fun.
3 I don't like arguing with friends.
4 I hate being late for a meeting.
5 I'm afraid of going out alone at night.
6 He's nervous about getting engaged.

Section 4
Paragraph 1
a) Males usually fly there from Mexico or Central America before the females.
d) As soon as they arrive, they begin to look for a mating place.
b) It's important for the male to establish his territory around their mating place and guard it against intruders.

Paragraph 2
f) The most important method of attracting the females is to fly around energetically.
e) The males fly high up into the air, and then dive straight down back toward the ground again.
c) Other strategies include singing and flapping their wings as fast as possible to create a loud humming sound.

Section 5
Exercise A
1 T 2 F 3 T 4 F 5 T 6 F

Section 6
Exercise A
1 c 2 f 3 a 4 b 5 d 6 e

Exercise B
1 Did you get hungry?
2 Did you get tired?
3 Did he get angry?
4 Did you get sick?
5 Did he get better?
6 Did you get thirsty?

Read and write
Exercise A

	What did they do on their first date?	How did they feel?	What would they prefer to do on a first date?
Gloria	went to a Chinese restaurant and ate noodles with chopsticks	shy, nervous	eat Mexican food or pizza
Takeo	went bowling	bored	go to a concert

DOWN TIME
Exercise A
1 Sue and Tim got back together again.
2 Sue and Tim got married.
3 Sue and Mike went on a date.
4 Sue and Tim broke up.
5 Tim asked Sue out.
6 Sue and Tim got engaged.

Exercise B
1 hungry 2 thirsty 3 angry 3 bored
5 better 6 scared 7 married
Mystery word: romance

UNIT 9

Section 1
Exercise A
1 snows 2 windy 3 sunny 4 stormy 5 foggy 6 rains

Exercise B
1 cold, snow 2 sunny, cloud, hot
3 cold, cloudy, rain, wet, windy 4 cold, foggy, stormy

Exercise C
1 snow 2 raining 3 stormy 4 wind 5 rain 6 cloudy

Section 2
Exercise A
1 will 2 may 3 will 4 might 5 will 6 might

Exercise B
1 We might go swimming this weekend.
2 I'm sure it won't rain today.
3 We may get a lot of snow this winter.
4 I will definitely go to the beach next weekend.
5 They might not go on vacation this year.
6 It will probably be sunny tomorrow.

Exercise C
Possible answers:
1 a) He may/might not find a new job.
   b) He will get some good advice.
2 a) They will go into the store.
   b) They might/may buy a new dress.
3 a) She will not/won't finish her work today.
   b) She may/might be very tired when she goes home.

Section 3
Exercise A
1 Excuse me, can I interrupt you for a second?
2 Excuse me, can I ask a quick question?
3 Sorry to interrupt, but what was the homework?

Exercise B

	Topic of main conversation	Reason for interrupting
Conversation 1	making copies	borrow a pen
Conversation 2	having lunch	ask the way to the cafeteria
Conversation 3	getting information about courses	get a copy of the class timetable

Section 4
Exercise A
1 forest 2 hill 3 mountain 4 sea
5 lake 6 river 7 island 8 field

Exercise B
1 island 2 lake 3 mountain
4 sea 5 river 6 forest

Section 5
Exercise A
1 T 2 T 3 F 4 T

Exercise B
1 b 2 a 3 a 4 b 5 a

Section 6
Exercise A
1 c 2 b 3 a 4 b 5 a 6 c

Exercise C
1 are, going to do
2 'm not going to drive
3 're going to save
4 Will, be
5 won't be
6 'm going to join
7 are, going to do
8 're going to make
9 'm going to ride
10 'm not going to use
11 'll do

Listen and write
Exercise B
Person 1: Picture 2
Person 2: Picture 3
Person 3: Picture 1

Exercise C

	1	2	3
Country/City	small island, Greece	Tuscany, Italy	Manhattan, New York City
Natural features / Climate	beach, warm and sunny, clear blue sea	hills, fruit trees, hot summers, warm winters	
Advantages		peace and quiet	won't need a car, good public transportation, cheap places to eat
Disadvantages		lonely	noisy, expensive
Lifestyle activities	morning: go out and catch fish, afternoon: take a nap under a palm tree	live on a farm, grow olives, grow vegetables and flowers	go out to the theater and art exhibitions, eat out every day

DOWN TIME
Exercise A
1 snow 2 island 3 mountain 4 sunny 5 weather

Exercise B
Across
1 island 3 forest 6 mountain 7 clouds / cloudy
Down
2 storms / stormy 4 sunny 5 windy 8 lake

UNIT 10

Section 1
Exercise A
1 have 2 gift 3 decorate 4 guests 5 snacks 6 play

Exercise B
1 invited 2 guests 3 snacks 4 made
5 decorated 6 music 7 gift 8 conversation

Section 2
Exercise A
1 to book a room   4 to buy a new dress
2 to reserve a flight   5 to buy some new shoes
3 to get some money   6 to pack her bag, to rest

Watch out!
She went to Mexico to see her friend.

Exercise B
1 in order to increase   4 in order to let
2 in order to help   5 in order not to disturb
3 in order not to take   6 in order not to make

Section 3
Exercise A
1 crowded 2 relaxed 3 awful 4 lively 5 soft 6 fun

Exercise B
1 Atmosphere: relaxed   2 Atmosphere: lively
Music: soft   Music: loud

Section 4
Exercise A
a

Exercise B
1 c 2 a 3 b

Section 5
Exercise A

Strongly agree	Agree	Disagree	Strongly disagree
I completely agree.	Yes, that's right.	I don't think that's right.	I don't agree.
You're absolutely right.	Yes, that's true.	I'm not sure I agree.	That's not true.

Exercise B
1 agree 2 disagree 3 agree

Exercise C
1 I completely agree.
✗ I don't agree.
2 I'm not sure I agree.
✗ That's not true.
✗ Yes, that's right.
✗ Yes, that's true.
3 You're absolutely right.
✗ I don't think that's right.

Section 6
Exercise A
1 f 2 a 3 c 4 b 5 e 6 d

Exercise B
1 am having, I'll
2 are you going to, We're having
3 We're going, are you going to
4 leaves, It won't take
5 are you doing, I'm going to

Exercise C
1 does, start
2 are, going to wear
3 'll/will wear
4 'll/will have
5 are, going to make
6 'll/will bring
7 isn't coming/isn't going to come
8 's working
9 's going
10 'll/will be

Watch out!
Are you staying at home tonight? / Are you going to stay at home tonight?

DOWN TIME
Exercise A
empty – crowded   quiet – noisy   new – old
large – small   short – tall   stressful – relaxing

Exercise B
boring – dull   lively – exciting   small – tiny
huge – enormous   noisy – loud   terrible – awful

Exercise C
1 loud 2 terrible 3 empty 4 snacks 5 happy
6 small 7 lively 8 large 9 awful 10 guests 11 noisy
Mystery message: Let's have fun!

UNIT 11

Section 1
Exercise A
1 wood 2 glass 3 rubber 4 ceramic
5 metal 6 plastic 7 cotton 8 nylon

Exercise B
1 plastic
2 wood/metal/plastic
3 cotton/nylon/plastic
4 cotton/nylon
5 glass/plastic/metal/rubber
6 wood/plastic/metal/glass/ceramic

Section 2
Exercise A
1 P 2 A 3 A 4 P 5 P 6 A

Watch out!
The table is made of wood.

Exercise B
1 is sold 2 is manufactured 3 are made
4 aren't recycled 5 Are, produced 6 is used

Exercise C
1 Plastic and glass are not recycled in my country.
2 Solar energy is used to generate electricity.
3 Computers are used to control the temperature.
4 Cell phones are sold in electronics stores.
5 This app can be downloaded onto your smartphone.

Section 3
Exercise A
b

Exercise B
1 b 2 c 3 a 4 a 5 a

Section 4
Exercise A
1 was taken 2 was made 3 was invented
4 were developed 5 were sold

Exercise B
1 When was the World Wide Web created?
It was created by Tim Berners-Lee in 1989.
2 When were the first iPhones® produced?
They were produced in 2007.
3 When was the Apple® logo designed?
It was designed by Rob Janoff in 1977.
4 When was the computer mouse invented?
It was invented by Douglas Engelbart in 1963.

Section 5
Exercise A
1 back up 2 click 3 install 4 log on
5 type in 6 right-click 7 print out 8 add

Exercise B
1 log on 2 type in 3 install 4 right-click
5 print out 6 click 7 back up 8 add

Section 6
Exercise A
1 printer 2 laptop 3 smartphone 4 coffee machine

Exercise B
3 I guess so. 1 I think … 1 I'm not sure…
3 Maybe. 4 I suppose so. 2 … probably …

Listen and write
Exercise A
1 T 2 F 3 T 4 F 5 DS 6 T

Exercise B
1 in touch with friends   4 reviews of restaurants
2 directions   5 pictures
3 times of shows or movies 6 music

DOWN TIME
Exercise A
1 B, L; microwave 2 A, J; cell phone 3 C, E; hair dryer
4 D, H; mouse 5 G, K; laptop 6 I, F; game console

Exercise B
glass   metal   rubber
cotton   ceramic   plastic
Mystery gadget: camera

UNIT 12

Section 1
Exercise A
1 f 2 d 3 c 4 e 5 b 6 a

Exercise B
1 admire 2 have arguments 3 make up
4 get along with 5 share the same values 6 go through

Section 2
Exercise A
1 b 2 b 3 a 4 b 5 a 6 a

Watch out!
If you <u>help</u> me, I will help you.

Exercise B
1 have, try 2 get, don't 3 don't, ask 4 will find, talk
5 give, will get 6 will try, call 7 doesn't, won't
8 won't be, go

Exercise C
1 If I <u>don't</u> have breakfast, I can't concentrate.
2 You will feel tired if you <u>don't</u> get enough sleep.
3 We won't get to school on time if we <u>don't</u> leave now.
4 Our parents get worried if we <u>aren't</u> home on time.

Section 3
Exercise A
1 d 2 c 3 e 4 a 5 f 6 b

Exercise B
1 Job security 4 help my community
2 job satisfaction 5 have power
3 having good friendships 6 hard work

Section 4
Exercise A
agree

Exercise B
1 agree 2 disagree 3 disagree 4 agree

Exercise C
5 Actually, I think you're right.
3 I'm not sure about that.
6 Exactly.
2 Yes, that's true.
1 Well, I think …
4 I think you're forgetting that …

Section 5
Exercise A
1 had 2 Would 3 could 4 wouldn't 5 would
6 wouldn't 7 would 8 were

Section 6
Exercise A
1 It is an opportunity to get real-life experience.
2 They can think carefully about what they want to study at college.
3 They can travel to other countries, or find a job.
4 It can be a lot of fun.
5 It helps young people develop confidence and maturity.

Exercise B
Suggested answer
Many young people take a year off before they start college. It is an opportunity to get real-life experience. For example, they can travel to other countries, or find a job. Also, they can think carefully about what they want to study at college. In addition, it helps young people develop confidence and maturity. Finally, it can be a lot of fun.

Read and write
Exercise A
1 T 2 T 3 F 4 F 5 F 6 T

DOWN TIME
Across
2 share 3 adventure 8 argument 9 power
Down
1 friendship 3 admire 4 community
5 get 6 make 7 security

Exercise B
1 friendship 2 independence 3 money
4 power 5 security 6 family 7 love

NOTES